AmericanGirl Library®

Bright Ideas

From Girls, For Girls!

Illustrated by Susan Synarski

PLEASANT COMPANY
PUBLICATIONS ™

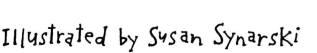

Published by Pleasant Company Publications
© Copyright 1997 by Pleasant Company

First Edition. Printed in the United States of America.
97 98 99 00 01 02 03 WCR 10 9 8 7 6 5 4 3 2 1

American Girl Library® is a trademark of Pleasant Company.

Editorial Development: Trula Magruder, Michelle Watkins
Art Direction: Kym Abrams
Design: Ingrid Hess
Photography: Mike Walker, Fritz Geiger, Tosca Radigonda,
Paul Tryba, Alan Shortall
Craft Styling: Nancy Gardner, Anne Lepley Wilkins, Kerry Vitali

Portions of this book have been previously published in
American Girl® magazine.

Library of Congress Cataloging-in-Publication Data
Bright ideas : from girls, for girls! — 1st ed.
p. cm.
Summary: A collection of activities for girls including crafts,
recipes, moneymaking projects, party games, and more.
ISBN 1–56247–527–4
1. Girls—Juvenile literature. 2. Creative activities and seat
work—Juvenile literature.   [1. Handicraft.]   I. Pleasant Company
Publications. HQ77.B65 1997 305.23—dc21 97–19933 CIP AC

Dear American girl,

This book is bursting with fun, fresh, creative ideas from girls like you! We dug through the *American Girl* magazine mailbag and tapped into our Web site to find girls' brightest ideas for crafts, games, recipes, money-makers, and much more.

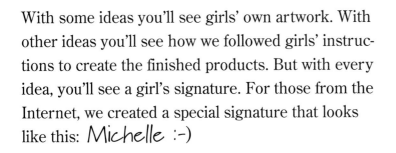

With some ideas you'll see girls' own artwork. With other ideas you'll see how we followed girls' instructions to create the finished products. But with every idea, you'll see a girl's signature. For those from the Internet, we created a special signature that looks like this: Michelle :-)

We hope you'll be inspired to try out each idea and give it your own special twist. But most of all, we hope you'll send us more suggestions. A lot of American girls are waiting to hear your bright ideas!

Sincerely,
Your friends at *American Girl*

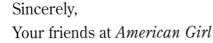

Contents

PET-A-MANIA
Lauryn W.
Please call
555-1234

PET-A-MANIA
Lauryn W.
Please call
555-1234

School Smarts

Style File

Fun and Games

Crafty Creatures

What's Your Bright Idea?

Chocolate Champ

In a parfait glass pour a layer of **hot fudge,** then add chocolate chip **ice cream,** more hot fudge, then chocolate ice cream, more hot fudge, and finally chocolate fudge ice cream. Top with **malted milk balls,** then add **chocolate whipped cream.** Sprinkle with **chocolate chips.** Add chocolate **wafers** and a **cherry.**

California

Homemade Stamp

To make homemade stamps, cut camper-mount **foam** (available at hardware stores) into different shapes or letters. Pull off the foam's **paper** backing and stick it to a block of **wood.** Press the stamp onto an **ink pad** and then press it to your **paper!**

Molly R.
California

Enviable Envelopes

Tory H.
Connecticut
Tory's envelope is out of this world!

Megan Z.
Pennsylvania
Megan makes the world a letter place!

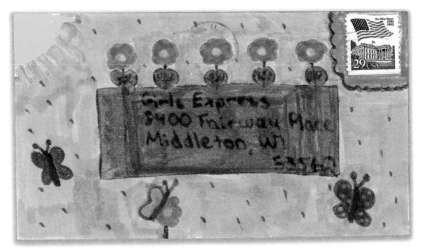

MANDIE W.
Illinois   Mandie's mail is in fine bloom.

Angela J.
Oregon   Angela sends news in hues!

Lindsey H.
Illinois   Lindsey writes thumbody a letter.

Rainy Day Fun

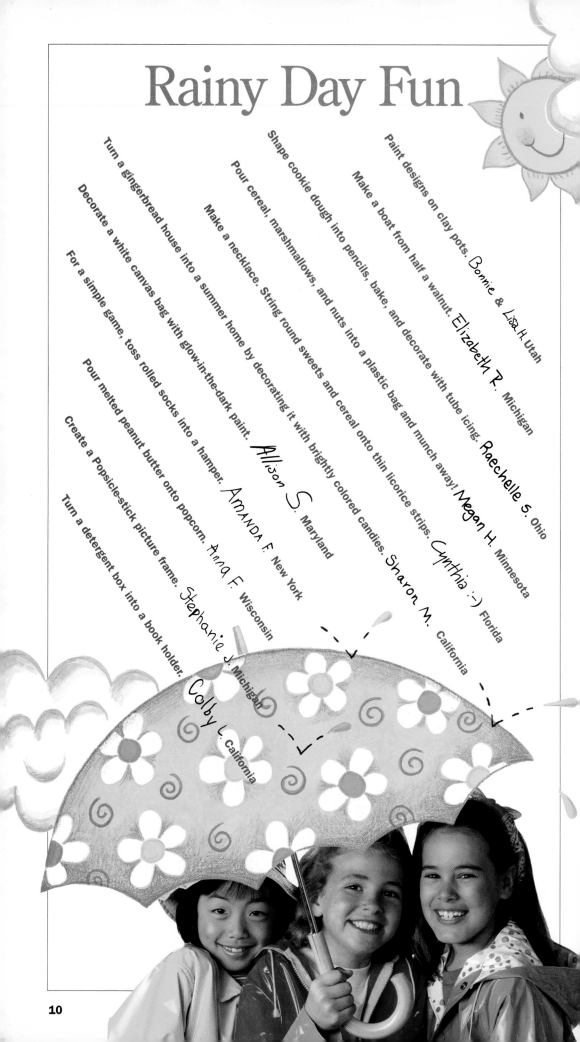

Paint designs on clay pots. Bonnie & Lisa H. Utah

Make a boat from half a walnut. Elizabeth R. Michigan

Shape cookie dough into pencils, bake, and decorate with tube icing. Raechelle S. Ohio

Pour cereal, marshmallows, and nuts into a plastic bag and munch away! Megan H. Minnesota

Make a necklace. String round sweets and cereal onto thin licorice strips. Cynthia :-) Florida

Turn a gingerbread house into a summer home by decorating it with brightly colored candies. Sharon M. California

Decorate a white canvas bag with glow-in-the-dark paint. Allison S. Maryland

For a simple game, toss rolled socks into a hamper. Amanda F. New York

Pour melted peanut butter onto popcorn. Anna F. Wisconsin

Create a Popsicle-stick picture frame. Stephanie J. Michigan

Turn a detergent box into a book holder. Colby L. California

10

Create a smile file! Cut out funny pictures, jokes, or riddles and stick them into a photo album. When you're feeling sad, grab the smile file to turn your frown upside down!

New York

Pocket Bugs

To make a pocket bug, polish a **stone** with a **rag.** Use **paint markers, googly eyes,** and other items to create the bug. I like making ladybugs. Hold the stone carefully so the ink won't smear. To make a bug shiny, coat it with clear **nail polish.** Let dry. Make legs or antennae with **wire,** and **superglue** them on.

alice Cl.
Michigan

Multiply a Butterfly

Cut out a **paper** heart and **color** a design. Fold the heart in half. Lay a pipe cleaner along the fold, then bend it over the top and down the back. **Superglue** it down and cut off the extra pipe cleaner. To make antennae, bend a **wire** into a V and slip it under the pipe cleaner. Make lots of butterflies—just be set to grab your net!

Nichole L.
Tennessee

Add an Animal

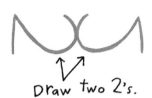

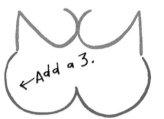

Draw two 2's.

Add a 3.

Finish with a nose, eyes, a bow, and whiskers!

Make a **cat** from two 2's.

Danielle J.
Louisiana

Draw a 4.

Connect a 3 to the 4.

Add a nose, an eye, an ear, and a tail. Color it in!

Make a **mouse** from 43.

Susan B.
Massachusetts

Draw a 2.

Add a beak and a body.

Finish with an eye and tail feathers!

Make a **swan** from a 2.

Jessica B.
New York

Wacky Words

I love figuring out wacky words. Here are some of my favorites. I hope you like them.

Illinois

Stick People

At the top of a **Popsicle stick** or wider craft stick glue on **googly eyes.** Add a smile with a **marker.** Design a dress, shirt, or other clothing from **felt, fabric, ribbon,** or **paper.** Glue the clothes to the stick. Glue **embroidery floss** on top of the stick for hair!

Lisa G.
Illinois

Quick Quilt

Put **newspaper** under a **paper towel** and outline squares with a silver **marker.** Fill in each square with a different brightly colored **marker** and let it dry. Now wrap your doll in a quilt made by you!

Esty a.
Connecticut

Zippy Dips

Two-Fruit Dip
Mash together 2 bananas and an avocado and eat with chips.

Lindsay C.
Florida

Zippy Chip Dip
Mix equal parts sour cream and salsa.

Carina S.
Massachusetts

Pretzel Dip
Melt a cup of chocolate chips in the microwave, and then dip in mini pretzels. Be careful! The chocolate might be hot. Lay pretzels on wax paper and freeze.

Camber :-)
Utah

Dainty Dip
Mix equal parts strawberry yogurt and whipped cream. Use as dip for plain or chocolate-covered strawberries.

Sara C.
New Jersey

Thick Dip
Dip apple slices into peanut butter and then roll them in Rice Krispies.

Teri H.
New Jersey

Apple Dip
Blend 8 ounces cream cheese with ½ teaspoon vanilla, 1 cup crushed peanuts, and ¾ cup brown sugar. Mix well.

Kristen L.
Pennsylvania

Throw an unbirthday party! Invite friends for a dinner to celebrate being one day older. Exchange gifts. It's everyone's unbirthday. Today comes but once a year!

Robyn :-)
Colorado

Bitty Burgers

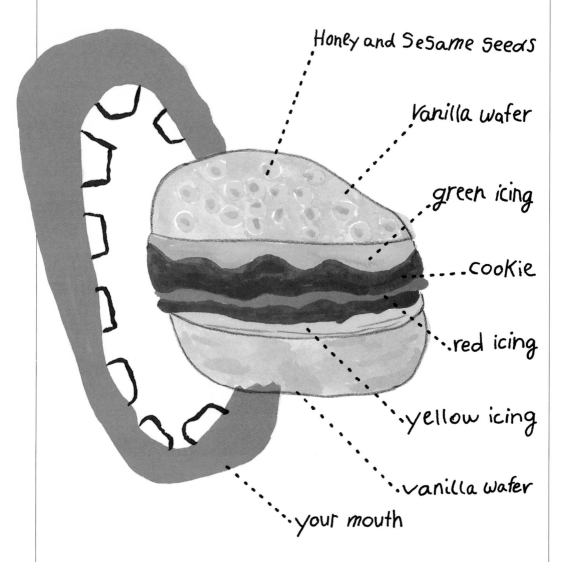

Honey and Sesame Seeds

Vanilla wafer

green icing

cookie

red icing

yellow icing

vanilla wafer

your mouth

To make these tiny burgers, spread green **icing** on the flat side of a **vanilla wafer** and yellow icing on the flat side of another wafer. Place a chocolate-covered **cookie** between the wafers. Squeeze a line of red icing around the chocolate cookie. Spread a thin layer of **honey** on the top wafer, and then sprinkle on **sesame seeds.**

Marie E. Rachie W.

California

Funky Fries

Place two slices of **bread** in the toaster. Toast until brown. Remove the crusts. Butter the toast and sprinkle it with **cinnamon** and **sugar.** Cut the bread into strips. Put a blotch of red **icing** on the plate to be the ketchup, and *voila*, funky French fries!

Cheryl :-)
Arizona

Savvy Sports Tips

Soccer Spy

Soccer practice gets boring. So I pretend I'm James Bond and the ball is a secret package I must deliver to the FBI. I imagine the trees, bushes, and other things in my yard are people trying to stop me! Before I know it, I'm playing better!

Stacy G.
Michigan

Bubble Gum Baseball

When I first started to play softball, I could hear other team players chattering at me, which made me nervous! Then I began to chew gum. It kept me focused and made me less nervous. I even blow bubbles at bat! Now lots of us bring gum to the games!

Hannah E.
Oklahoma

Team Spirit

Team swimming requires practice—which can be boring and discouraging. It helps to play mind games, like singing "I have only three laps left . . ." to the tune of "Twinkle, Twinkle, Little Star."

Emily S.
Wisconsin

Game Point

To be better at tennis, you need lots of practice—especially with serves. Set goals. Say, "I'm going to make ten serves in a row into the forehand service court." Then stick with it!

Erin S.
Texas

Rings

Make a ring for every finger with **twist ties!**
Peel the **paper** or **plastic** off a twist tie. String
a pattern of **beads** onto the bare **wire.** After
the beaded wire reaches around your finger, twist
wire ends together and cut off any extra wire with
scissors. Don't make it too tight! Make some
for your friends, too.

Kate :-)
Texas

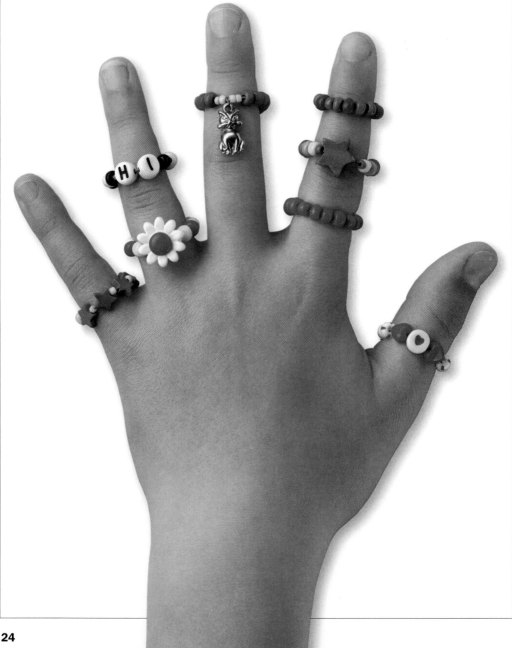

Brighten up! Try stamps on colored laces.

Print a pattern with alternating stamp colors.

Add sizzle with a mix of markers and stamps.

Make your mark with markers!

Strings

Personalize your **sneakers** with these crazy laces! Lay a pair of white cotton **shoelaces** onto a piece of **paper.** Using mini **stamps,** like the Crayola brand, stamp a pattern on both sides. Let dry. Then string up your sneakers!

Jenny L.
New Jersey

Clothespin Cuties

This craft is easy and fun to do! To make this doll, you need an old-fashioned **clothespin.** Cut a dress or other clothing from scraps of **fabric,** and glue it onto the doll. Glue a **ribbon** to her head. Design a face with **markers.** Now you have an all-American doll for an all-American girl!

Laura F.
New York

My friends and I make keepsake bookmarks! Sometimes we decorate the bookmarks using the themes from the books that our friends are reading!

Rachel R.
Florida

Ready to Recycle

Make party paper by scattering confetti onto pulp!

Use old newspaper to create a natural color.

Press on doilies for a pretty valentine!

Don't toss out your **old paper**—recycle it! Recycled paper is great for birthday cards, for very personalized letters to friends, and to keep on hand for your own special projects.

Felicity L.

California

An adult to
help you
- Scissors
- Used paper, about 5 sheets
- 3 cups of water
- Blender
- Screen with very fine mesh
- Plastic tub

1 Cut the paper into ½-inch squares. Note: unless you're mixing paper colors, your recycled paper will be the same color as your original paper.

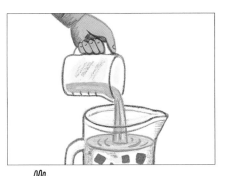

2 Pour water and cut paper into the blender. Puree until smooth. Mixture should be about as thin as gravy. If it seems too thick, add more water.

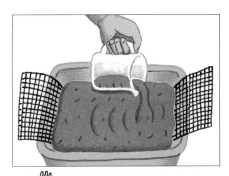

3 Slide the screen into the tub. Pour the pulp onto the screen. Note: If your screen is unmounted, ask an adult to help you. It can cut fingers!

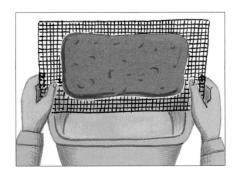

4 Lift up the screen. Shake it to distribute the pulp. The thinner the pulp on the screen, the thinner your paper will be.

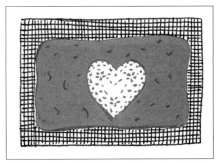

5 At this stage, add any extras you want—flowers, glitter, or embroidery floss. Set the screen aside to dry. Be careful where you place the screen— the pulp will be messy.

All Heart Bring a ham sandwich cut like a heart to school. Add watermelon, Red Hots, and punch. Put it in a white bag covered with heart stickers! *Justina W.*
Arkansas

Lovable Lunches

Sea Food Core half an apple and fill with tuna salad. Thread a cheese "sail" onto a toothpick, and stick it into the apple "boat." Serve with goldfish crackers and saltwater taffy. *Lydia Z.*
France

Peanut Passion For lunch, bring a peanut-butter-and-jelly sandwich, celery with peanut butter, a bag of peanuts, and peanut butter balls!

Julie S.
California

Care Bears Mom made my lunch with a peanut butter sandwich cut like a bear, bear-shaped cookies, and gummy bears. She put in a note that said, "Have a *beary* nice day!"

Nicole G.
New Jersey

HAVE A BEARY NICE DAY!

Bow Beauty

My sister and I have an idea for a hairbow holder. With **fabric, buttons, yarn,** and old **hairbows,** we made something pretty to hang in our bedroom or bathroom. It was lots of fun to make!

Laudan R.
Iowa

YOU WILL NEED

- Cloth or yarn scraps
- 18-by-18-inch piece of cloth
- Rubber band
- Fabric glue
- Assorted buttons and sequins
- Scissors
- Hair-colored yarn
- 2 matching hairbows

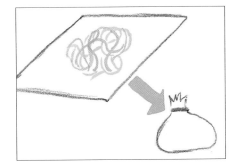

1 Put a large handful of scrap cloth or yarn into the middle of the cloth square. Gather the 4 corners and wrap tightly with a rubber band. Make sure all the stuffing is inside.

2 On the flat side, glue on buttons for the eyes and a button for the nose. Glue on buttons or sequins for the mouth and rosy cheeks.

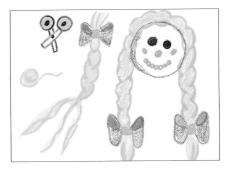

3 Cut sixty 30-inch pieces of yarn. Tie them together at one end with a bow. Next, split the hair into 3 equal sections. Braid the yarn. Attach a second bow. Glue the braid on as shown.

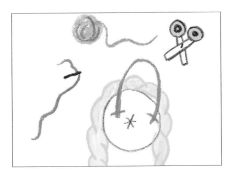

4 Cut a 12-inch piece of yarn. Sew or hot-glue the ends of the yarn onto the fabric in back to hang up your holder.

5 Now clip your bows and barrettes onto the long braids to use when you need them!

Great Games

Backseat Blast

Before the trip, riders make a list of 20 things they expect to see while traveling. As they see an item on their list, they check it off. The person with the most items checked off wins.

Sharon :-)
Missouri

Crazy Relay Race

Each team has four players: a frog, a horse, a rabbit, and a girl. Frog leaps to tag horse. Horse gallops to tag rabbit. Rabbit hops to tag girl. Girl dances to the finish line!

KATIE ROSE H.
Florida

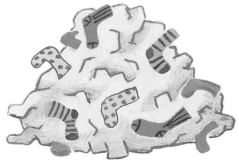

Knee Highs

Each player or team of players gets a balloon. Players keep their hands behind their backs and use their knees to keep the balloon in the air. The player whose balloon touches the floor last wins.

Hannah E.
Illinois

Spot the Sock

Build a mountain of socks of all sizes and colors. As each player matches a pair of socks, she keeps them beside her. When all the socks are gone, the player who has the most matches wins!

Annie J.
Washington, D.C.

My brother loves bubbles. So I took a bowl, poured in bubble solution, and dipped in a flyswatter! It sounds pretty crazy, but it made lots and lots of beautiful bubbles!

Bethany D.

Virginia

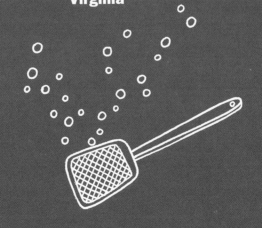

At Your Service

Wash and Shine

Hold a door-to-door car wash and/or dog wash! Another idea: polish silver for parents and neighbors!

Lindsay R.
Arkansas

Recycling Makes Cents

Separate plastics, aluminum, and paper for people who recycle. Be sure both you and your parents know your clients.

Jessica L.
California

Party Favor

Offer to babysit guests' kids during your parents' parties. You can charge $1 an hour per kid. Most parents tip!

Kate C.
California

Picture Perfect

Set up a card table and sign for face painting. Kids don't have a lot of cash, so charge only 25 cents a painting.

Taylor V.
Michigan

Help at Home

Try babysitting children while their parents are home! They can get work done—you can earn money and get training!

Jordy R.
New York

FOR SALE

Lemonade with a Twist

Skip the lemonade stand this year and sell slushies! Freeze lemonade in ice trays. Crush the cubes. Place into Styrofoam cups. Put the cups into a cooler and pack with ice. Before serving, pour in extra drink. Sell for 25 cents!

Emily S.
Pennsylvania

Pebble Peddler

Sell painted rocks! On a flat rock, paint a person's name plus a flower or design using poster paints. Use these as samples. Sell the rocks for 50 cents!

Vanessa K.
Pennsylvania

Art Smart

Hold an art fair on your front lawn! Gather up your friends to create paintings, drawings, sculptures, and other crafts to sell.

Toby :-)
Virginia

Kids R Us!

This garage sale is all for kids! Serve 10-cent snacks and drinks. Play music. Sell old toys, books, clothes, stuffed animals, even your old bike—all at reasonable prices. Before the sale, hang fliers with date, time, and place.

Stephanie V.
New York

A Cuddly Career

My ten friends and I started a Pet-a-Mania club. We put up **fliers,** handed out **business cards,** and told people we would walk, sit, or bathe their **pets.** Word spread. Now all members of Pet-a-Mania are busy. It's a great way to earn **money** and have fun!

Lauryn W.
Texas

Perky Puppy

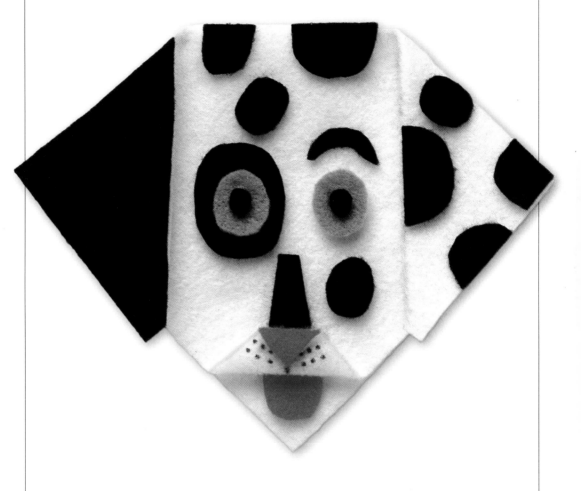

Create a puppy in seconds! Fold a square sheet of **paper** or **felt** in half so it looks like a triangle. To make ears, fold down the top corners. To make a nose, fold up the top layer from the bottom and then fold it down again (see above). If using felt, **glue** down the ears and nose. Now decorate your dog. You can even make a pet parade!

Jessica S.

Connecticut

Crack a Code

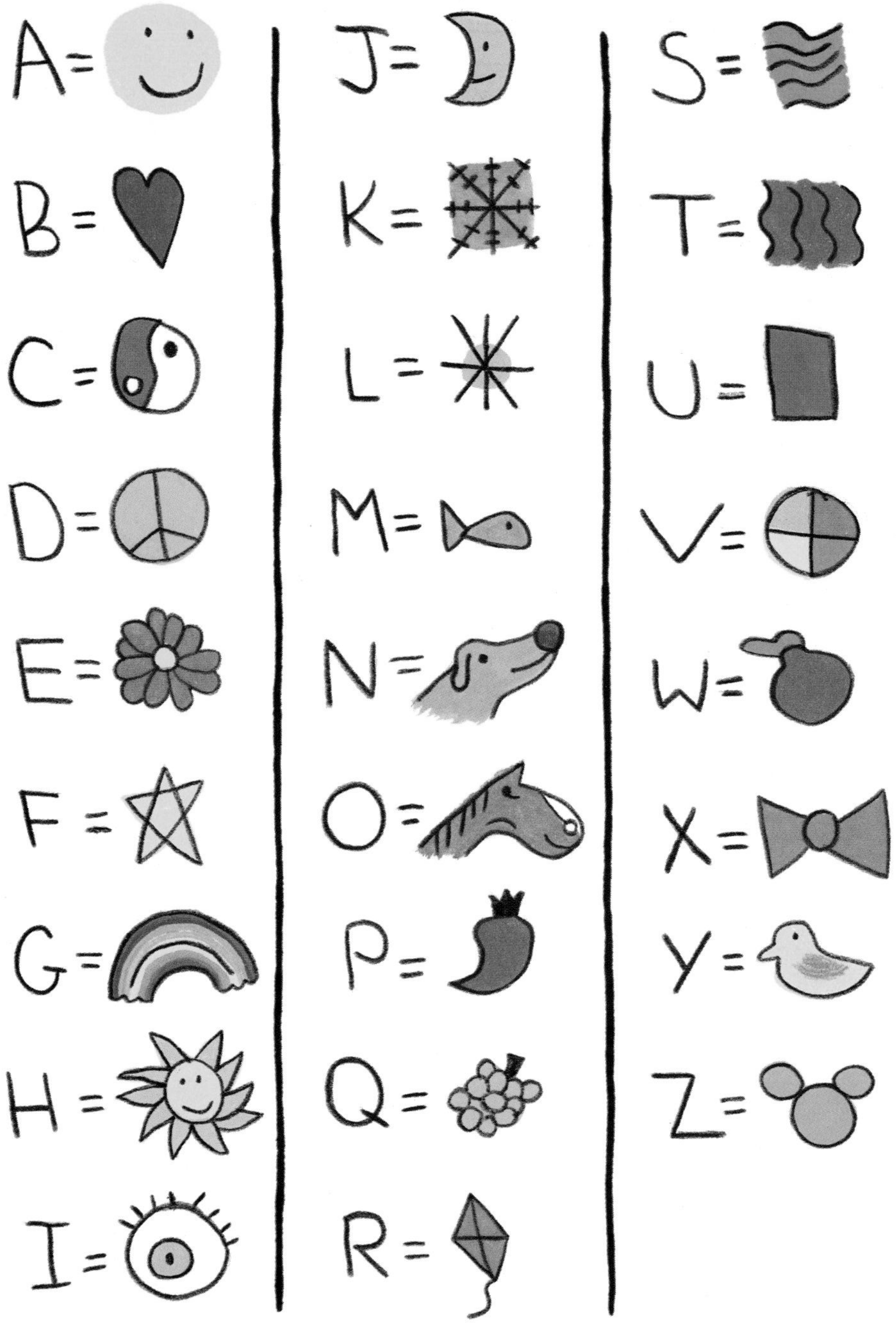

A = 😊
B = ♥
C = ☯
D = ☮
E = 🌸
F = ⭐
G = 🌈
H = 🌻
I = 👁

J = 🌙
K = ✳
L = ✴
M = 🐟
N = 🐕
O = 🐴
P = 🦃
Q = 🍇
R = 🪁

S = 〰
T = 〰〰
U = ▪
V = ⊕
W = 🎈
X = 🎀
Y = 🐤
Z = 🐭

Here's our **secret code.** You can make your own or use ours. Use our code to solve this riddle!

Adrienne F.   Samantha S.
Maxine S.
Texas

Why did the turtle cross the road?

Cool Party Picks

At your next slumber party, have a midnight **tea party!**
Elizabeth :-)
Washington

Design a party **board game!** On paper, draw a path of squares for spaces. Decorate the board with a theme, like fun facts about your friends! Glue the paper onto cardboard, collect dice and game pieces, and play!

Lauren :-)
Ohio

Make a **tent** in your room with old sheets. Read books that will scare the pants off everyone!

Colleen :-)
New Jersey

For your next slumber party, tell your friends to come dressed in their pajamas so you can start having fun, fun, fun—immediately!

Leah :-)
California

Miss Twist

With a few items from around your house, you can make a cute collection of people! You will need **pipe cleaners, fabric, thread, glue, scissors, yarn,** and lots of imagination!

Nancy F.
Pennsylvania

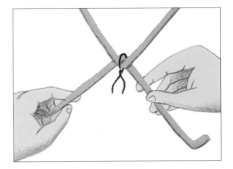

1 Bend a pipe cleaner into an upside down V. To make "feet," bend the ends outward ½ inch. Link a second V pipe cleaner through the top of the first V. Wrap thread around both of them several times and tie a knot.

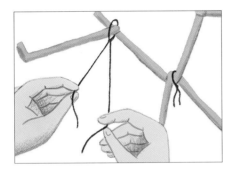

2 Cut a third pipe cleaner in half. Twist each half around the ends of the top pipe cleaner to make "arms." Tie these on, then bend the ends of the arms into "hands."

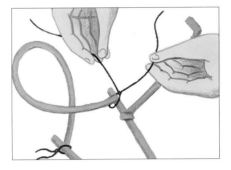

3 To make a head, tie the fourth pipe cleaner to the end of the left "shoulder" with thread. Bend and loop the pipe cleaner over to the other side, and tie it with thread to the right "shoulder."

4 Cut out a 6-by-10-inch piece of fabric. Fold it in half. Cut a 1-inch slit along the fold for the head. Trim the fabric as desired to make clothing. Slip on the fabric. Glue the edges together.

5 Make hair from yarn and attach with thread as shown.

A Special Report

For a book report, I made a fake TV using a **box** as the screen and a **hanger** as the antenna. In class I placed the box over my head and pretended to be a reporter discussing the characters in the book!

Jessica D.
Maryland

POWER

A+ Reports

Book Bash

I threw a party for a character in the book I had read, *Claudia: The Genius on Elm Street*. I had invitations, fudge—everything!

Allison D.
California

Read All About It!

For a book report, I designed a huge, colorful newspaper! I created a comics section, an editorial page, a feature article, and even a Dear Abby column—all based on events in the book. It looked really nice.

Rebecca P.
California

Body Building

For my report, I made a human body. I cut her from cardboard, made her lungs from pink sponges, and created her organs from fabric that I stuffed and sewed. I attached the organs to the body with Velcro. I filled two books writing about each system. I titled them *The Body Book: The Inside Story*!

Gina A.
Illinois

Dolled-Up Clips

Cut a piece of **fabric** to fit around a **paper clip** like a dress, and then **glue** it on. Next, glue on **googly eyes.** Make lots of these dolls. Before you go to bed, tell each of your "worry dolls" a different trouble. They'll fix them while you sleep!

Jessica Kelli Lauren
Jackie Tiffany
Kansas

Summer Sips

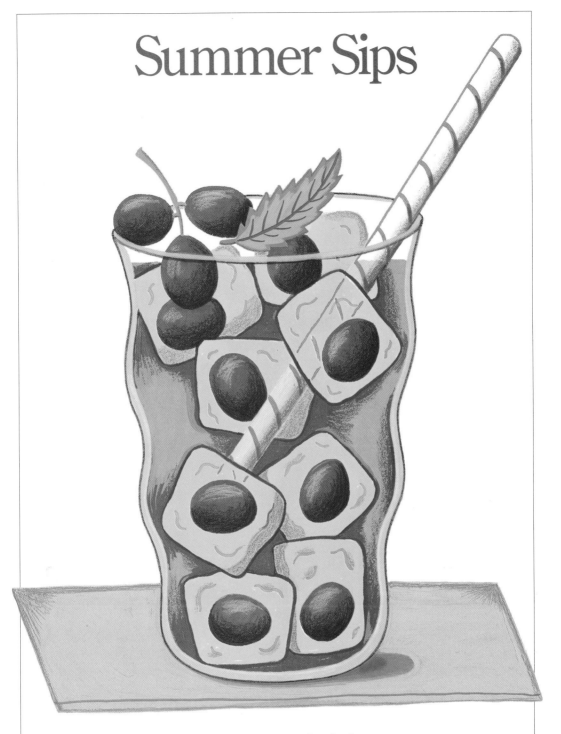

Fill an **ice tray** with **apple juice.** Put one **grape** into each section of the tray. Freeze. Put the ice cubes into a glass of **punch.** When the juice is gone, crunch, crunch, crunch!

Stephanie :-)
Georgia

Four Seasons of Fun

Spring Fling Chalk Challenge

Go to a sidewalk or other area of concrete. Each person writes her **initials** with chalk as many times as she can in two minutes. The player who writes the most wins.

Kasey K.
Mississippi

Duck, Duck, Splash

Play this game like Duck, Duck, Goose, only the person who is **It** carries a glass of cold water. **It** says, "Drip, drip . . ." as she sprinkles water on the heads of those seated. When she gets to someone she wants to be **It,** she dumps the entire glass of water on her and yells, "Splash!" The one splashed chases **It** back to her spot in the circle.

Natalie :-)
Missouri

Back-to-School Pencil Roll

Each player gets on her hands and knees and tries to roll a pencil across the floor using only her **nose.** The first one to the finish line wins.

Stephanie F.
Oklahoma

Snow Pile Scramble

Two or more people stand at the bottom of a big pile of snow. On the word go, you all scramble to the **top** without using your hands. If your hands touch the snow, you must go back to the bottom. The first one up wins!

Becky R.
Massachusetts

A Day with Dad

See the *Nutcracker* **ballet** and then shop
for a special nutcracker.

Taylor :-)
California

Take a **canoe trip** and camp by the river.

Amanda :-)
Pennsylvania

Make **pancakes** together.

Colby :-)
Dubai, United Arab Emirates

Have a **secret word.** Say it throughout
the day to each other!

Sara :-)
Massachusetts

Once a month have a **father-daughter day.**
Do something special.

Naomi :-)
Ohio

A Day with Mom

Garden together in the summer.

Allison :-)
California

Take long **drives.** Ask her to let you decide
which way to go!

Cheryl :-)
Washington

Hit the beach! Have a **picnic** and build
a sand castle.

Kayla :-)
California

Rent a scary **movie,** cuddle up, and get
scared together!

Lauren :-)
New York

Take oil painting **lessons** together. It's a fun
way to spend time, and you learn something cool!

Ali :-)
Mississippi

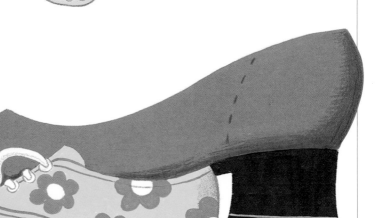

Easy Embossing

YOU WILL NEED

- An adult to help you
- Stamp
- Ink pad
- Paper
- Embossing powder (available at craft stores)
- Iron or lightbulb
- Marker

1 Press the stamp onto the ink pad, then onto a piece of paper.

2 Sprinkle embossing powder onto the stamp before the ink dries, then pour the extra powder back into the jar.

3 With an adult's help, press the back side of the stamped paper close to a hot surface, such as an iron or lightbulb, until the powder melts and becomes shiny.

4 Mix embossed stamps with markers, try different colors of embossing powder, or leave it as it is. Ta-da! You have a finished picture.

Katrissa S.
Illinois

Super Stationery

Sally Anne Smith
100 Parkway Place
New York, New York

Write or type an address on a peel-off **label** (available at office supply stores). Then, using **fabric paint,** decorate the label with flowers, hearts, anything! Dry completely. Now you can send a letter with an embossed label!

Jennifer W.
New Jersey

Cut out stars, hearts, or any shape from **wrapping paper.** Paste the cutouts onto paper with a **glue stick.** Decorate **envelopes,** too!

Rachel S.
Pennsylvania

Sally Anne Smith
100 Parkway Place
New York, New York

Maria Anderson
450 Lincoln Lane
Austin, Texas 91234

A Kiss for You

Get a jump start on making valentines for your family! Cut out a card from brown construction **paper** that looks like a Hershey's Kiss. Write a message on it that says something like "A Kiss for you on Valentine's Day." Wrap **aluminum foil** around the paper, and give it to someone you love!

Erin :-)
New Jersey

Make time fly with a countdown calendar chain! Create a paper link for each day until a big event. Tear off one link per day. Before long, you'll be 24 hours away from your big day!

Robin :-)
British Columbia

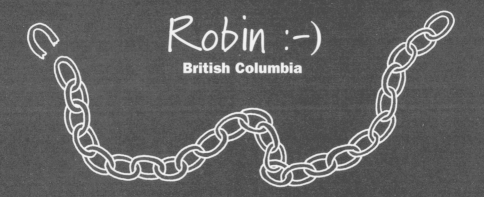

Bunny Buddies

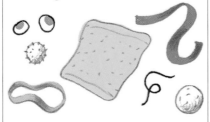
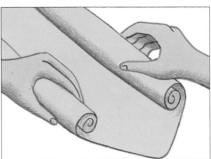

1 Spread a washcloth onto the table. Tightly roll 1 corner toward the center of the cloth. Holding this rolled section firmly, turn the washcloth around and roll the other corner into the center.

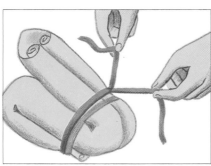

2 Fold the washcloth in half so the rolls face up. Hold these tightly! Fold the bottom end under about 2 inches. To make a head, wrap the rubber band around the front, including the bottom fold. Tie ribbon around the rubber band.

3 To make a face, glue on large googly eyes. Dab fabric glue onto the center of the face, then press on embroidery floss for whiskers. Glue on pom-poms for the nose and tail.

Natalie A.
New York

Clever Costumes

Pippi Longstocking

Ask an adult to bend a hanger to fit over your head and stick out evenly on both sides. Then braid the hanger into your hair. To make mismatched tights, cut one leg off two pairs of old tights, then pull on both pairs. Finally, dot on freckles!

Sarah K.
New York

Grump

Wear a bathrobe, mess up your hair, hold a coffee mug, and wear a sign around your neck that says "I'm not a morning person!"

Emily T.
Washington

I'M NOT A MOrNING PERSON!

A Dollar Bill

Use cardboard to make a giant dollar bill. Cut out a hole in the center. In back, attach a piece of fabric loosely over the hole. Dress up like George Washington. Now stick your head in front of the fabric and look out the hole!

Natalie B.
Illinois

Friendship Necklace

Cut out a heart. Stencil "best friends" on the heart. Cut a zigzag down the middle. Make a paper chain so you and a friend can each wear a piece around your neck!

Kara O. Virginia M.
California

Friends Forever

You and a friend dress identically, and then slip on one oversize shirt! It's hard walking together, but it's lots of fun!

Rachel C. Livia L.
New Jersey

Autograph Book

Wear a large white shirt and sweat pants. Bring a marker when you go trick-or-treating. Ask people to sign their names!

Rebekka G.
Washington

A Fancy Frame

Every year my friends and I wear festive attire
and have our pictures taken as a group. We frame
our photos and decorate the frames with **fabric,
bows, ribbons, lace,** and even **glitter
paint.** Then we hang them on the Christmas
tree. I now have a collection from past years!

Beth B.
Illinois

A Merry Moose

We decorate our tree with these ornaments because we often have moose in our backyard. To make a moose, fold up the ends of a **pipe cleaner** and shape them into feet. Make a second pair, then drape the legs over a **dog biscuit.** Glue another biscuit to the top and a third biscuit in front for the head. Make a face, antlers, and a hat from pipe cleaners!

Katie C.   Hollie C.
Alaska

Do you have an idea
for a project, recipe,
moneymaker, or craft
you'd like to share?
Send your ideas to:
Bright Ideas
American Girl Library
8400 Fairway Place
Middleton, WI
53562

Or visit our Web site at
http://www.americangirl.com